Contents

Words that appear in **bold** can be found in the glossary on page 30.

🐾 The Environment Detective, Sherlock Bones, will help you learn about energy and how to use it wisely. The answers to Sherlock's questions can be found on page 31.

What is energy?

Energy is the force which makes things work. There are many different forms of energy, such as heat, light and electricity. People and animals get energy from their food.

Energy can be stored, for example, in a battery or a lump of coal. Energy can also change from one form to another. When you burn coal, stored energy is released as heat and light. Most of the energy on Earth comes from the Sun. Plants use sunlight energy to live and grow. Wood and coal are both made from plants. Plants also provide food for people and animals. You need energy from your food to move your muscles and stay alive.

Fuels are materials that can be burned to provide energy. A fuel may be a solid, liquid or gas. Wood and coal are solid fuels. Oil is a liquid fuel. Many machines run on electricity, which is mostly made by burning fuel.

ECO-FACTS

Fuel at home

Several different types of fuel provide heat and energy in our homes. Cookers use gas or electricity. The boiler that heats water for central heating may run on these fuels or oil or coal. You may have an open fire or a stove which burns wood or coal. Cars use petrol, diesel or kerosene, which are made from oil.

Our homes contain lots of gadgets which use energy.

🐾 **Can you list the items in this picture that use energy?**

THE ENVIRONMENT DETECTIVE INVESTIGATES

Using Energy Wisely

Jen Green

WAYLAND

6000204707

First published in 2010 by Wayland
This paperback edition published in 2012 by Wayland
Copyright © Wayland 2010

Wayland
Hachette Children's Books
338 Euston Road
London NW1 3BH

Wayland Australia
Level 17/207 Kent Street
Sydney NSW 2000

Editor: Katie Powell
Designer: Stephen Prosser
Maps and artwork: Peter Bull Art Studio
Sherlock Bones artwork: Richard Hook
Consultant: Michael Scott, OBE

British Library Cataloguing in Publication Data
Green, Jen.
  Using Energy Wisely. -- (The environment detective
investigates)
  1. Energy conservation--Juvenile literature. 2. Energy
  development--Environmental aspects--Juvenile literature.
  I. Title II. Series
  333.7'916-dc22

ISBN: 978 0 7502 6784 7

With thanks to Marine Current Turbines Ltd for the use
of the image on page 19.

Printed in China

Wayland is a division of Hachette Children's Books,
an Hachette UK Company,
www.hachette.co.uk.

Picture Acknowledgments:
The author and publisher would like to thank
the following for allowing their pictures
to be reproduced in this publication:
Cover © Istock, title page © Istock, imprint
page © Istock, 4 © Bubbles Photolibrary /
Alamy, 5 © Construction Photography/Corbis,
6 © Ronnie Kaufman/Blend Images/Corbis,
7 © Istock, 8 © Wayland, 9 © Craig
Lovell/Corbis, 10 © Istock, 11 © Wayland,
12 © WpN/Photoshot, 13 Robert
Landau/Corbis, 14 © Wayland, 15 © Getty
Images, 16 © Istock, 17 © Istock,
18 © Xiaoyang Liu/Corbis, 19 © Marine
Current Turbines Ltd, 20 © Bertrand
Gardel/Hemis/Corbis, 21 © Jack Sullivan /
Alamy, 22 © AFP/Getty Images, 23 © Istock,
24 © Britt Erlanson/Getty Images, 25 ©
Shutterstock, 26 © Strauss/Curtis/Corbis,
27 © Andersen Ross/Getty Images, 28 ©
Photoshot, 29 © Istock

The workman on the left is using energy from food to power his muscles. The other worker is using a roadroller, powered by diesel fuel.

Nowadays, huge amounts of energy are needed to run all the machines we use in daily life. But using so much energy causes problems. Fuels such as oil are running out. Burning fuels, such as coal, for energy produces **pollution**, which is harming the planet. New, less harmful, kinds of energy are being developed, but we also need to use energy more wisely. This book will explain all about energy and how we can save it.

DETECTIVE WORK

Make a list of all the types of fuel used in your home. Do you have an open fire or stove which burns coal or wood? What fuel is used for the central heating and cooker? If your family has a car, what fuel does it use?

How do we use energy?

Homes in villages, towns and cities use a lot of energy. This is called **domestic** use. Every family uses energy for light, heat, and to run all the equipment we use at home. Offices, farms and factories require huge amounts of energy, too.

The main form of energy we use at home is electricity. Cables carry electricity from power stations where it is made to cities where it is supplied to homes. Almost every room in the house has sockets where electricity is available at the flick of a switch. More than 50 per cent of all the energy we use at home goes on heating. Another 25 per cent is used to heat water for washing. The rest goes on equipment such as televisions, computers, kettles, microwaves and washing machines.

DETECTIVE WORK

Kitchens **consume** more energy than any other room in the house, because we use so many machines to prepare and cook our food, and clean up afterwards. Many kitchens also contain washing machines. Make a list of all the things that use energy in your kitchen.

Kitchens, like this one, contain all sorts of appliances that use a lot of energy.

Huge amounts of energy are also used on transport. Cars, buses, trains, ships and aircraft carry people from place to place. Trucks, boats and planes are also used to transport **raw materials** and finished goods across the world. Vehicles give off waste gases that cause a lot of air pollution. Traffic, especially private cars, also causes congestion on motorways and in city centres, particularly during rush hours.

Cars containing just one or two people produce far more pollution than public transport such as buses and trains, in which many people can travel. People travelling on a train produce just one third as much pollution as they would have done travelling by car.

Although the people caught in a traffic jam aren't moving, these cars are still causing pollution.

ECO-FACTS

Air travel

Air travel causes a lot of pollution. More than 200 million people now travel by plane each year and scientists believe that that figure could double in the next 30 years. One hundred people travelling 100 kilometres by car produce nearly 15 kilograms of the waste gas **carbon dioxide** (CO_2). One hundred people travelling the same distance by plane produce even more pollution, more than 18 kilograms of carbon dioxide.

Who uses energy?

People in different parts of the world use very different amounts of energy. People in the United States use more energy in a day than people in less developed regions, such as Africa, would use in more than two weeks.

In more developed countries, such as the United Kingdom and the United States of America, machines such as cars, computers, televisions and washing machines do our work for us, or provide entertainment. We consume huge amounts of energy each year. In countries such as the United States, where fuel is plentiful, a lot of energy gets wasted. The world's developed nations consume about 70 per cent of all the energy used each year, even though they have just 25 per cent of the world's **population**.

ECO-FACTS

Car use in the United States and China

In the United States, there are 765 cars for every 1,000 people. This one country uses more than 40 per cent of the world's total oil use on its vehicles. The United States has 4.5 per cent of the world's population. In China, there are just 131 cars for every 1,000 people, but car use in China is rising fast. China has nearly 20 per cent of the world's population. If as many Chinese as Americans had cars, there wouldn't be enough oil to go round.

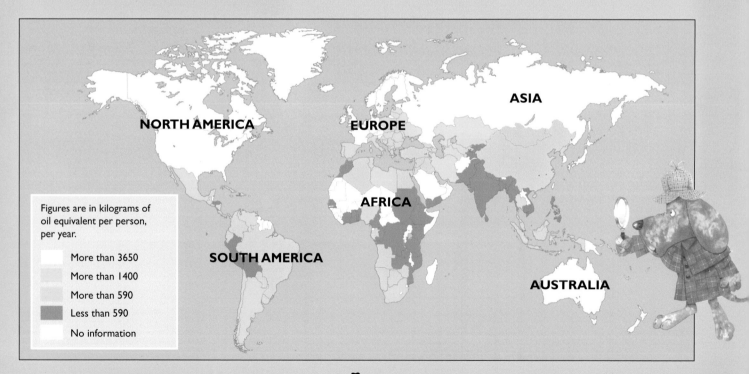

Figures are in kilograms of oil equivalent per person, per year.

- More than 3650
- More than 1400
- More than 590
- Less than 590
- No information

NORTH AMERICA

EUROPE

ASIA

AFRICA

SOUTH AMERICA

AUSTRALIA

This map shows how much energy is used per person in different parts of the world.

Can you name one region where people use a lot of energy and another region where little energy is used per person?

In China, many people use bicycles instead of cars to get around, but car use is increasing.

In less developed regions, such as many African countries, people use a lot less energy. There are fewer machines and people have less money to spend on energy. Fuels such as wood or **dung** are burned to provide energy for heating and cooking, and people wash clothes by hand. However, the population is increasing rapidly in many of these areas. Countries such as India and China are also developing their industries very quickly. People here want the machines that make life comfortable and these use lots of energy. New factories and power stations open every week, so energy use in these areas is rising quickly.

DETECTIVE WORK

Find out where the electricity meter is located in your house and take a reading. There may be two figures, for electricity charged at different rates by day and night. Take another reading a week later. Subtract the first figure from the second to work out how much electricity your family used in a week. This is recorded in kilowatt-hours. Divide it by the number of people in your house to find out how much you each use. A typical person in Bangladesh uses 36 kilowatt-hours in a week. How does your family compare?

What are fossil fuels?

Most of the energy we use comes from coal, oil or natural gas. These fuels are called **fossil fuels** because they are made of plants or animals that lived and died millions of years ago, and later became fossils.

Coal is not a rock, but the solid remains of giant tree ferns that grew in swampy forests more than 250 million years ago. When these tree-like plants died, the trunks crashed to the ground and were buried under more **vegetation**. Heat and pressure slowly turned the remains to coal. Oil and gas are the remains of sea creatures that lived in prehistoric oceans. When they died, their remains were buried by debris on the seabed. Over millions of years they were crushed and decayed, and slowly turned to oil or natural gas.

Oil rigs drill into the seabed to reach oil, which is then pumped to the surface.

ECO-FACTS

Made from oil

Oil is widely used in manufacturing, including to make plastic. Different kinds of plastic are used to make toys, machines and anything from bottles to bags and trays. Clothes made from nylon, polyester and other fabrics are also made from oil. So are synthetic rubber products, from car tyres to wellington boots.

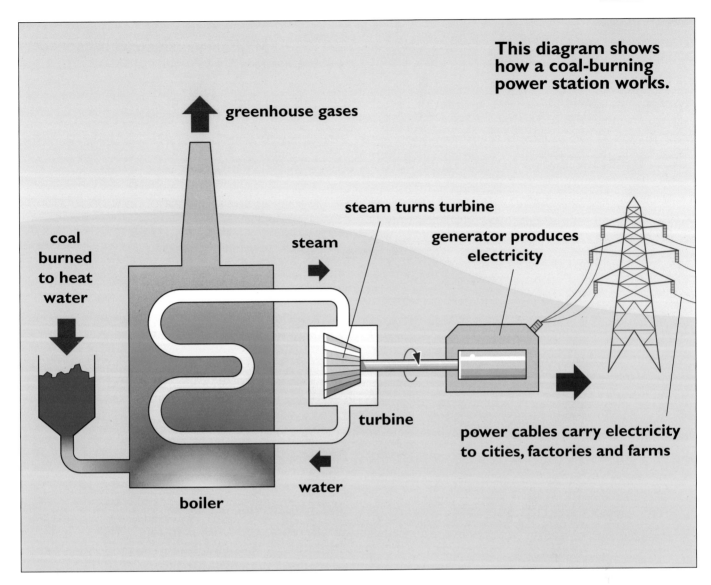

This diagram shows how a coal-burning power station works.

greenhouse gases

coal burned to heat water

steam

steam turns turbine

generator produces electricity

turbine

water

boiler

power cables carry electricity to cities, factories and farms

Today, coal, oil and natural gas are found underground beneath land or in the seabed. Mines, oil wells or oil rigs are used to bring the fuel to the surface. It is then transported by tanker, truck or pipeline to the places where it is needed.

Coal, oil and gas are the main fuels burned in power stations to produce electricity. In a coal-burning power station, coal is burned in a boiler to heat water. The water turns to steam, which spins a machine called a **turbine**. The turbine drives a **generator** which produces electricity.

Fossil fuels have been used to power machinery since the late 1700s. Oil is also processed to make fuels such as petrol, diesel and kerosene. These are used to run vehicles from cars and buses to trains and planes.

DETECTIVE WORK

Look around your bedroom and make a list of all the things made from oil. The information in the Eco-facts box will help you. Don't forget to count clothing made of synthetic fabrics such as nylon or polyester! You can find this information by looking at the labels in your clothes.

What are the problems with using fossil fuels?

Fossil fuels provide most of the energy we use at home and school, and to travel from place to place. However, these fuels are becoming scarce. Burning fossil fuels also produces pollution, which is harming the natural world.

Stocks of fossil fuels are limited. They are only found in certain areas and once they are used up, they cannot be renewed, or replaced. For this reason they are called **non-renewable** fuels. Experts believe the world's oil stocks will only last 40 or 50 years. Natural gas will last 70 years or so. Coal will last longer, perhaps another 300 years, but one day it, too, will run out. We need to find alternatives to using fossil fuels.

🐾 **By 2150 what types of fossil fuel will probably have run out? What fuel will be left?**

ECO-FACTS

Climate change

Global warming is affecting the Earth's climate. Many dry places seem to be getting even drier, while some wet areas are being hit by floods. Violent storms seem to be striking more often. These changes are making farming more difficult in some areas.

As sea levels rise due to global warming, flooding is becoming common on low-lying islands such as Kiribati, in the Pacific Ocean. Salt water is harming plants and the soil.

When fossil fuels are burned, carbon dioxide gas is released. This gas is building up in the **atmosphere** and trapping too much of the Sun's heat. This is called the **Greenhouse Effect** because carbon dioxide acts like the glass in a greenhouse. The gases that cause the warming are called **greenhouse gases**, and they are making Earth slowly heat up, a problem called global warming. As the oceans get warmer, they expand, which is making sea levels rise, along with extra water from glaciers melting in the heat.

When fossil fuels are burned, waste gases are given off. These waste gases mix with water vapour in the air to produce rain that is slightly acidic. **Acid rain** can kill trees and enter lakes to harm water life. Waste gases given off by cars and power stations react with sunlight to produce a dirty haze called **smog**. This hangs over many cities and can harm people's health.

DETECTIVE WORK

Test the Greenhouse Effect. Using a thermometer, take a reading of the air temperature on a sunny day. Now put the thermometer in a greenhouse, conservatory or on a sunny window sill. Take the temperature again after 15 minutes. Carbon dioxide in the atmosphere has a similar effect to the glass of a greenhouse on the air temperature.

Smog hangs over the city of Los Angeles, in the United States. Dense smog can make it hard for people to breathe.

What are the alternatives to fossil fuels?

Around the world but especially in developed countries, our use of fossil fuels is harming the planet. We need to turn to other sources of energy that don't damage the atmosphere. **Nuclear energy** and **biofuels** are two alternatives.

Country	Percentage of total energy	No. of nuclear power plants	No. of plants being built or planned
US	20	104	15
UK	13.5	19	4
China	2	11	33
Japan	25	53	15
France	76	59	2
Germany	25	17	0

This table shows the numbers of nuclear power plants in different countries, and the amount of energy they provide.

✿ **Which country has the most nuclear plants? In what country does nuclear power provide the greatest percentage of energy used?**

Nuclear energy is made by processing the rare mineral uranium in special power stations. Uranium is made of tiny **particles** called **atoms**. In a machine called a **reactor**, these atoms can be split into even smaller particles. This process releases heat which can be used to make steam. The steam spins turbines which **generate** electricity, in a similar way to steam in coal-burning power stations.

Nuclear power stations don't produce greenhouse gases, but they do produce very dangerous **radioactive** waste, which is a problem to get rid of. Nuclear waste remains harmful for thousands of years. Scientists haven't worked out how to deal with it, so most of the waste is sealed in concrete and buried underground. Some people feel this is storing up trouble for the future. Supplies of uranium are limited, so this fuel is also non-renewable and will eventually run out.

ECO-FACTS

Ups and downs of nuclear power

The first nuclear power plant opened in Britain in 1956. By the 1980s, many countries were using nuclear energy. However, in 1986, a serious accident at the Chernobyl power plant in Russia spread radioactive waste over a vast area. Most countries stopped building nuclear reactors. However, since 2000, many countries have restarted their nuclear programme because they are even more worried about the dangers of burning fossils fuels.

Biomass is a natural material that comes from plants and animals. Dung, crop waste and fast-growing plants like willow or sugar-cane are all types of biomass. These natural fuels can be burned to produce energy. If these materials are allowed to rot in a special tank, they produce methane gas, which can also be burned to provide energy. Burning biofuels releases some carbon dioxide, and methane is another greenhouse gas. However, growing plants for biofuels uses up as much pollution as it creates, so these fuels are truly **renewable**.

Small biogas plants like this one produce enough energy for a house or farm. Large biogas stations can provide energy for a whole city.

DETECTIVE WORK
Contact your electricity company or log onto the company's website. What energy sources are used to produce the electricity you use? What percentage does nuclear energy provide?

What is 'clean' energy?

Natural forces such as sunlight, wind and volcanic activity can be used to produce energy. These sources provide what is known as 'clean' energy because they produce far less pollution than fossil fuels or nuclear power.

The Sun is Earth's main energy source. The Sun's heat drives the weather and allows life to flourish on Earth. **Solar** technology uses the Sun's energy in several different ways. Solar panels on the roofs of houses heat water for families to use. Other panels called **photovoltaic panels** change sunlight into electricity. Small items of equipment, such as torches and calculators, can also run on solar power.

People bathe in a warm pool near a geothermal power plant in Iceland.

ECO-FACTS

Geothermal energy

In volcanic areas, such as Iceland and New Zealand, hot rocks lie close to the surface. Natural underground water bubbles to the surface as hot springs. Water can also be pumped down from the surface, heated and piped back up to warm houses. Or the hot water can be used to produce steam and generate electricity. **Geothermal energy** is renewable, but it does produce some greenhouse gases.

How do you think this natural pool is heated?

The strong ocean winds mean wind farms at sea produce 30 per cent more energy than on land.

Solar energy is a renewable energy source. However, while solar panels provide cheap energy they are quite expensive to buy, and they don't produce energy at night. Scientists are working on new ways to store solar energy to make it more efficient.

Wind energy has been used for centuries. Since ancient times, windmills have been used to grind grain to make flour. Modern wind turbines consist of a tall column with two or three blades. The blades turn in the wind to spin the turbine, which is linked to a generator. Like solar power, wind energy is renewable, but the turbines need to be located in windy places. Some people feel they look ugly and spoil the countryside, so they are sometimes sited out at sea.

DETECTIVE WORK

Wind turbines produce clean, renewable energy, but some people feel they are not very attractive, and are also noisy. Ask your friends and family what they think about wind turbines. Would they be happy about having a wind turbine nearby? Record the results in two columns, for and against.

How can water provide energy?

Flowing water is another source of energy which will last as long as rivers flow to the sea. Like wind power, the energy of swift-moving rivers has been used for centuries. More recently, scientists have developed ways of **harnessing** the energy of waves and tides.

Energy generated from streams and rivers is called **hydroelectric power** – HEP for short. The rushing water is channelled past turbines which spin to work a generator and produce electricity. Hydroelectric energy is clean and renewable. However, HEP stations often damage the environment. A dam is usually built to speed up the flow of water. A reservoir forms behind the dam. This alters the valley upstream, destroying an area of natural **habitat** and harming wildlife. Sometimes towns and villages are drowned by the lake.

ECO-FACTS

The Three Gorges Dam

Very large HEP schemes can affect a huge area. In 2007, a huge hydroelectric plant was completed in China. A dam 185 metres high was built across the Yangtze River in the scenic Three Gorges area. The reservoir formed by the dam is 650 kilometres long. The scheme generates a huge amount of energy, but 1.2 million people had to move to make way for the dam.

The Three Gorges hydroelectric scheme in China has changed a scenic river gorge, which was once an important tourist attraction.

🐾 **Can you explain how the lake in the photo formed?**

Tidal power stations harness the energy of tides. In some of these plants, a dam called a **barrage** is built across the mouth of a river. As the tide rises, water flows through the barrage and is then trapped and released when the tide has fallen. Water surges past turbines to generate electricity. These stations generate clean, renewable energy but harm the habitat at the river mouth.
In more modern tidal stations a turbine shaped like an upside-down wind turbine is sited in open water in a strong tidal current, which is less damaging for wildlife.

Wave technology is still being developed. In some wave stations, waves are channelled up a ramp to force air past turbines. Wave energy is clean and renewable, but rough seas whipped up by storms can damage the equipment quite easily, and this can be costly to repair.

This new tidal turbine, called SeaGen, is located on the inlet of Strangford Lough in Northern Ireland.

DETECTIVE WORK
Imagine a new HEP station is planned on a river in your area. The scheme will generate energy for your city but will change the landscape and drown several villages. How would you feel about it? What would you say in a letter to the council?

What new forms of energy are being developed?

Energy produced from sunlight, wind and waves is clean and renewable, but these natural sources are not always reliable. Scientists around the world are working to develop new technology which will provide cheap, clean and reliable energy. Governments and private businesses are funding this vital research.

ECO-FACTS

Alternative fuels for cars

Cars that run on oil produce huge amounts of greenhouse gases. Now, scientists have developed vehicles that cause less pollution. Electric vehicles are recharged from mains electricity. Hybrid cars run on a mixture of oil and electricity. Solar cars have been developed. Cars that run on hydrogen or biofuels such as sugar cane are also on the roads.

In an ordinary battery, two chemicals react to produce an electric charge. **Fuel cells** work in a similar way to batteries, but use the reaction between two gases: **hydrogen** in the cell and **oxygen** in the air. The two combine to produce electricity, with only water as a waste product. Fuel cells produce no pollution, but hydrogen is difficult to store and harness. Now scientists have developed a fuel cell that uses natural gas, which is easier to work with.

In the past, electric vehicles were slow and often had to be recharged. New designs have overcome these problems.

✿ **Why do you think a hydrogen fuel cell produces water as well as energy?**

Ordinary batteries used in torches and radios contain harmful chemicals which cause pollution when they wear out and are thrown away. They also take a lot of energy to make. Now, rechargeable batteries are available. These can be charged over and over again using mains electricity, which cuts down on waste. However, mains electricity is mostly produced by burning fossil fuels. Wind-up technology is also available for torches and radios. You wind a spring which slowly uncoils, releasing energy. This technology produces no pollution as it runs on muscle-power!

Every day we produce rubbish and also **sewage**. Now, these limitless resources can be used to make energy! Rubbish can be burned in special **incinerators** to produce energy. However, the furnace has to be kept very hot, or harmful pollution escapes. Scientists in Japan have developed a way to produce energy from sewage. A factory changes sewage into **fuel slurry**, which can be burned instead of fossil fuels. These technologies are renewable but they do produce some greenhouse gases.

DETECTIVE WORK
Look around your home for new technology. Do you have wind-up or solar-powered torches, radios or calculators? Does your family have any gadgets that run on rechargeable batteries? Do you have solar panels or solar lights?

In European countries, waste incinerators like this one in Austria are an important source of heat and energy.

What is being done to save energy?

Three-quarters of all the energy we use comes from fossil fuels, which are becoming scarce and are also damaging the planet. Clean, renewable energy provides part of the answer, but we all need to use energy more carefully, and not waste it. Governments and **conservation** groups can show the way.

In the last twenty years or so, conservation groups such as Greenpeace have made people more aware of climate change and the problems with fossil fuels. Nowadays, many people are taking steps to save energy, for example by using the car less, or by taking a train instead of a plane for a long journey where possible.

Governments can help by making laws requiring all new houses to be energy saving, and by offering grants to help people ensure their homes lose less heat and waste less electricity. They can also help by providing good public transport, so people can use cars less.

DETECTIVE WORK

Find out about the work of conservation groups such as Greenpeace and Friends of the Earth by logging onto their websites, listed on page 31. Investigate what is being done in your local area to save energy and reduce pollution.

These Greenpeace supporters are taking part in a campaign to inform people about climate change.

Since the 1990s, governments around the world have met at conferences to try to agree cuts in greenhouse gases. Britain, Japan and many European countries have agreed to important cuts. However, despite all the pledges, the total production of greenhouse gases is still rising. In 1990, the world production of carbon dioxide was 21.3 billion tonnes. By 2000, this figure was up by 12 per cent to 23.8 billion tonnes. By 2003, it had risen another 7 per cent to 25.6 billion tonnes.

ECO-FACTS

Carbon-offsetting

Trees and plants absorb carbon dioxide and give off oxygen, which helps to keep the air healthy. By planting trees we can counteract the amount of carbon dioxide produced, for example, by a plane journey. This practice, called **carbon-offsetting**, helps but does not completely solve the problem. A flight adds carbon dioxide to the air today, whereas a tree will take 20–30 years to absorb the same amount of carbon.

Planting young trees like this one will help improve air quality by absorbing carbon dioxide.

🐾 **Did world production of carbon dioxide rise more steeply during 1990–2000 or 2000–2003?**

How can we save energy at home?

Overuse of energy is harming nature. Climate change and pollution are daunting problems, but they can be tackled if everyone gets involved. In more developed countries, we all need to change our energy habits, and use a lot less energy. That way, as less developed countries use more energy, pollution levels won't rise steeply.

Energy-saving begins at home. Leaving lights on in empty rooms wastes energy, so switch them off as you leave. Energy is also wasted when we leave items such as televisions and computers in standby mode. This uses almost as much energy as having the machines on, so it's best to switch them off completely. Save energy in the kitchen by waiting until you have a full load before you use the washing machine or dishwasher, and use low-temperature water cycles. Hang clothes outside to dry instead of using the tumble drier.

Leaving the fridge door open wastes energy. Always close the fridge after you have got what you want to eat!

ECO-FACTS

Low-energy lightbulbs

You can buy low-energy lightbulbs to save energy on lighting. These bulbs cost a bit more to buy than ordinary bulbs, but use only a fifth of the energy. They also last five times as long! It has been estimated that if every house in Britain used just three of these bulbs, it would save enough energy to cover the country's street lighting!

Always check where your food comes from. Buying meat, fruit and vegetables produced locally saves energy on transportation.

A lot of energy gets wasted on heating, especially in winter. A snug, well-**insulated** home saves a lot of energy. Ask your parents to make sure the loft is well-insulated, and fix draughty doors and windows. If you feel chilly, put on a sweater instead of turning up the central heating. You can also save energy used to heat water for a bath by taking a quick shower instead.

The food we buy at supermarkets has often travelled thousands of kilometres from where it is grown or processed. This uses enormous amounts of energy. Your family can save energy by buying locally-grown fruit and vegetables in shops or markets. Plastic bags given out at supermarkets also take energy to make. Save energy by reusing old plastic bags, or taking a canvas bag when you go shopping.

DETECTIVE WORK

Next time you go shopping, look at the labels on fruit and vegetables to see where they are grown. Look the countries up in an atlas to see how far away they are. Ask your parents to buy local produce whenever possible.

How can we save energy at school?

Energy savings can be made at school as well as at home. Good insulation, **recycling** and reducing car use for journeys to and from school can all make important savings. If every school in the country saved even a little energy, it would make a big difference to the environment.

Recycling saves energy and also helps to tackle the problem of litter.

Schools can waste huge amounts of energy on lighting, heating, or by leaving machines on standby – far more than just one home. Ask your teacher if your class can start an energy patrol. Turn off lights, computers and machines such as photocopiers when they're not being used. Check for draughty doors and windows. Is the heating set too high or does it blast out heat at times when it's not needed? Some schools have started charging anyone who wastes energy a small fine. The money can used to pay for equipment or a school trip.

Eco-friendly schools

Schools in many countries have made big energy savings. One school in Pennsylvania, in the United States, made a video about saving energy. An energy drive cut the school's energy bills by almost half! Some British schools have installed solar panels on roofs or in covered walkways. These provide energy for lighting and to run computers.

Carry out a survey in your class to find out how everyone got to school. Record the results under these headings: Car / School bus / Bus / Train / Walk / Bike. If pupils who come by car live close together, they may be able to share a ride.

Energy is used to make bottles, tins and wrappers for all the food and drink eaten at school. That energy is wasted if the empty containers are just thrown away, but many materials can now be recycled. Start a recycling scheme at your school if there isn't one already. Paper, cardboard, glass, cans and plastic bottles can all be recycled.

In the term-time, a huge amount of energy is used to get everyone to and from school. Car journeys use far more energy than public transport, especially if each car brings only one child.

Ask your parents if it is possible for you to take the bus or train, or bike or walk to school. Or can you make arrangements with another family to share a ride?

Walking to school keeps you fit, saves energy and cuts pollution.

Your project

I f you've done the detective work and answered all of Sherlock's questions, you now know a lot about energy! Investigate further by producing your own energy project. You could choose from the following ideas.

Practical action

- Make an action plan for saving energy at home. First, find out how much energy your family uses in a week by taking meter readings – see page 9. Now draw up an action plan on a large sheet of paper. Write down all the ways your family uses energy in one column. It might help to go from room to room, looking at equipment. Don't forget the lights and heating. Beside each item, say how you think energy is wasted, and how it could be saved. Make a column for family members to tick each time they save energy in the ways you have suggested. Take another reading a week later. How much energy have you saved?
- You could ask your teacher if your class can make a similar action plan for the school. How is energy wasted at school, and how can it be saved?

Topics to investigate

- Find out all you can about one particular energy source. It could be fossil fuels, nuclear energy or a renewable source, such as solar or wind power. How long have people been using this type of energy and where is it used? What are the advantages and disadvantages? Is it renewable and does it cause pollution?
- Find out more about how schools are saving energy using this website: www.eco-schools.org.uk/ Ask your teacher if your school can register for this scheme.
- Find out more about energy use in countries around the world using this website: www.nationmaster.com/graph/ene_com_ene_use-energy-commercial-use

Your local library and the Internet can provide all sorts of information. Try the websites listed on page 31.

Make a note of all the items in each room of your house that use energy.

Solar panels on the roof provide energy for heating and lighting homes.

Project presentation

- Imagine you are making a television documentary about energy. Make a plan showing the main points you want to talk about in the order that makes the most sense.
- People have different attitudes to energy, especially when their work is involved. You could write a short report about energy from the point of view of one of these people: an environmental campaigner, a coal miner, someone who works in a nuclear power plant or on an oil rig, a scientist researching new energy technology or a government official.

🐾 Sherlock has found out about how animals are used to provide energy for machinery or transport. Dogs are used to pull sledges in the Arctic. Horses and oxen pull ploughs while horses also carry people. All animals are fuelled by their food.

Glossary

acid rain Rain that is slightly acidic because of air pollution.

atmosphere The layer of gases that surrounds the Earth.

atom A tiny particle of matter.

barrage A type of dam.

biofuel Fuel made from natural materials, such as rotting plant waste.

biogas A fuel produced from natural materials.

biomass Natural materials that come from plants or animals.

carbon dioxide A gas absorbed by plants and given off by animals as they breathe.

carbon-offsetting When people give money to projects to counteract the greenhouse gases they cause.

conservation Work done to protect the natural world.

consume To use up.

domestic Belonging to the home.

dung Manure.

fossil fuels A fuel that is made of fossilised plants or animals that lived long ago. Fossil fuels include coal, oil and natural gas.

fuel A substance that can be burned or used up to produce energy.

fuel cell A machine that makes energy using a gas such as hydrogen.

fuel slurry A fuel made from sewage.

geothermal energy Energy made by using rocks heated by volcanic activity.

generate To produce something.

generator A machine which produces electricity.

global warming Rising temperatures worldwide, caused by an increase of gases in the atmosphere that trap the Sun's heat.

Greenhouse Effect The warming effect caused by certain gases in the air, which reduce how much of the Sun's heat escapes into space.

greenhouse gases Gases in the air that trap the Sun's heat. Carbon dioxide is a greenhouse gas.

habitat A particular kind of area where plants and animals live, such as a rainforest or desert.

harness To use.

hydroelectric power Energy made from fast-flowing water.

hydrogen A gas which produces water when combined with oxygen.

incinerator A hot furnace in which rubbish is burned.

insulate To prevent energy such as heat from escaping and being wasted.

non-renewable Refers to energy sources that are used up and cannot be replaced, such as coal or oil.

nuclear energy A form of energy that is made by splitting atoms of uranium.

oxygen A gas that makes up one-fifth of Earth's atmosphere, which animals use to breathe.

particle A tiny piece of matter, such as an atom or a grain of dust.

photovoltaic panel A solar panel which turns light into electrical energy.

pollution Any harmful substances that damage the environment.

population The number of people living in a country or area.

radioactive Refers to materials that decay naturally and give off dangerous radiation.

raw material A natural substance used in manufacturing.

reactor A machine where nuclear energy is made by splitting atoms of uranium.

recycling When waste is saved and remade into a new product.

renewable Refers to natural energy sources that can be replaced quickly by nature, so they are not used up.

sewage Dirty water from homes, containing chemicals and human waste.

smog A poisonous, dirty haze that forms in the air when polluting gases react with sunlight.

solar Of the Sun or sunlight.

turbine A machine driven by steam or water, which turns or spins.

vegetation The plants found in a particular habitat.

Answers

🐾 **Page 4:** A television, electric fire and a laptop computer.

🐾 **Page 8:** North America, western Europe, northern Asia, Australia and some countries in the Middle East use a lot of energy. Many countries in Africa, southern Asia and South America use relatively less energy.

🐾 **Page 12:** By 2150, oil and natural gas will probably have run out, unless new stocks have been discovered. There will still be coal.

🐾 **Page 14:** The United States has the largest number of nuclear power stations (104) but nuclear energy provides the greatest percentage of total energy in France (76 per cent).

🐾 **Page 16:** The pool is fed by a hot spring, produced by volcanic rocks heating underground water.

🐾 **Page 18:** River water held back by the Three Gorges Dam has built up to flood the land upstream.

🐾 **Page 20:** Water (H_2O) is made of hydrogen and oxygen. In the fuel cell, hydrogen combines with oxygen to make water and energy.

🐾 **Page 23:** In the ten years between 1990–2000, world production of CO_2 rose 12 per cent, giving an average rise of 1.2 per cent a year. In 2000–2003, the figure rose 7 per cent in just three years – an average of 2.3 per cent, so it rose faster in the second period.

Further information

Further reading

Let's Discuss Energy Resources series (Wayland, 2010)

Protecting Our Planet: Energy in Crises by Catherine Chambers (Wayland, 2009)

The Environment Atlas: Energy Resources by Meg and Jack Gillett (Wayland, 2010)

The Geography Detective Investigates: Pollution by Jen Green (Wayland, 2009)

Websites

Eco-schools, UK
www.eco-schools.org.uk/

Alliance to Save Energy: Green Schools program
http://ase.org/section/program/greenschl

US Dept of Energy website on saving energy
www.eere.energy.gov/kids/

Energy Saving Trust
www.energysavingtrust.org.uk/

Environment Protection Authority, Australia
www.environment.gov.au

The Young People's Trust for the Environment
www.ypte.org.uk/

Environmental factsheet from The Young People's Trust for the Environment
www.ypte.org.uk/environmental/environment-how-can-you-help-protect-it-/81

Greenpeace UK
www.greenpeace.org.uk

Friends of the Earth
www.foei.org

Worldwide Fund for Nature
www.wwf.org.uk

Index